Editor: Eve Marleau
Designer: Melissa Alaverdy
Picture Researcher:
   Maria Joannou

Copyright © QED Publishing 2010

Farmyard Friends Sheep
First published in 2011 by
Hinkler Books Pty Ltd
45-55 Fairchild Street
Heatherton Victoria 3202
Australia
www.hinklerbooks.com

10 9 8 7 6 5 4 3 2
16 15 14 13 12

ISBN 13: 9781741846942

All rights reserved. No part of this publication may be reproduced, stored in a retrieval system, or transmitted in any form or by any means, electronic, mechanical, photocopying, recording, or otherwise, without the prior permission of the publisher, nor be otherwise circulated in any form of binding or cover other than that in which it is published and without a similar condition being imposed on the subsequent purchaser.

A catalogue record for this book is available from the British Library.

Words in **bold** are explained in the Glossary on page 22.

Picture credits
(t=top, b=bottom, l=left, r=right, c=centre, fc=front cover)

Alamy Images Photogenix 11tl, Hazel Gwatkin 12t, Picture Partners 19t; **Corbis** Michael St. Maur Sheil 7t, José Fuste Raga 8-9, Anders Ryman 11tr; Getty Images Dorling Kindersley/Geoff Dann 20l; **Photolibrary** David Harrigan 5t, Sabine Lubenow 6-7, Nature Picture Library/Britain on View 8, Agustin Catalan 10t, Cotswolds Photo Library 15t, Robin Smith 16-17, Superstock 18l, Juniors Bildarchiv 21r, Roland T Frank 22-23; **Shutterstock** Eric Gevaert cr, Eric Isselée cl, cm, 2, Iakov Kalinin 2-3, MisterElements 3t, 5b, 6b, 11b, 12br, 15b, 16b, 18r, 20r, Eric Isselée 4l, 21l, 24b, Cen 4-5, Oxana Prokofyeva 6t, Walter Quirtmair 9t, Majeczka 10-11, Jean Frooms 12bl, Eric Gevaert 13t, 13b, Rickshu 14-15, Robyn Mackenzie 17t, F ranckreporter 18–19, Olly 24 (background).

Contents

What are sheep? 4
Sheep on the farm 6
Where do sheep live? 8
What do sheep eat? 10
The life cycle of sheep 12
The daily life of sheep 14
Why do we farm sheep? 16
Sheep shearing 18
Breeds of sheep 20
Glossary 22
Index 23
Notes for parents and teachers 24

What are sheep?

Sheep are mammals. All mammals have fur and drink their mother's milk when they are born.

A sheep's feet are called hooves. Each hoof is divided into two large toes. Most sheep have long white, cream, brown or black fur.

⇐ Sheep have thick fur called wool. It helps them to stay warm in the winter.

Sheep have large bodies and four thin legs. ⇒

hoof

toe

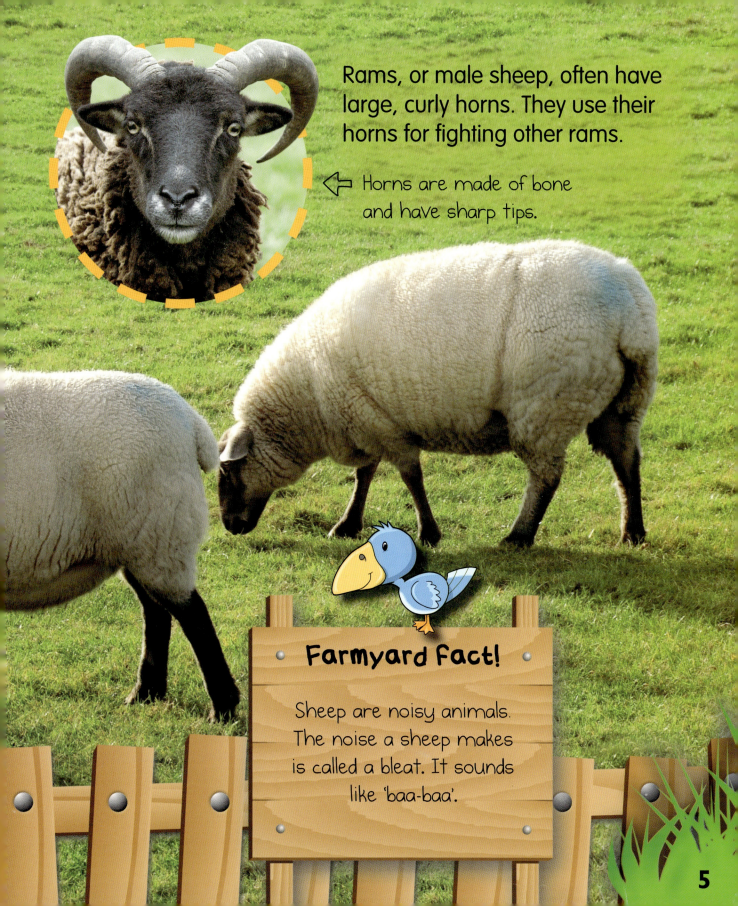

Rams, or male sheep, often have large, curly horns. They use their horns for fighting other rams.

⇐ Horns are made of bone and have sharp tips.

Farmyard Fact!

Sheep are noisy animals. The noise a sheep makes is called a bleat. It sounds like 'baa-baa'.

Sheep on the Farm

Farmers all over the world keep sheep for their wool, meat or milk. A sheep's wool is used to make clothing.

Most sheep are about 0.5 metres tall. That's about the height from the floor to your shoulder.

⇐ Female sheep and lambs are friendly animals.

⇓ Female sheep and lambs live together in flocks.

Farmyard Fact!

Sheep have lived on farms for thousands of years. They were probably one of the first animals that humans kept for food.

Sheep live in groups, called flocks. A female sheep is called a ewe. A male sheep is called a ram. Young sheep are called lambs.

Ewes are smaller than rams. Some ewes have horns.

Where do sheep live?

Most sheep live in pastures, or fields. Some sheep live on hills or mountains.

Sheep are tough animals that can live in all sorts of weather, from snow and rain to hot, dry conditions.

⇦ Their thick woollen coats help sheep to keep warm in snowy weather.

Sheep may be put in an area with a fence around it, called a **pen**. They can also be kept indoors. Farmers have to keep indoor pens clean, warm and dry.

Indoor pens protect sheep ⇨ from dogs and foxes that hunt them.

⇩ At the end of the day, the farmer puts his sheep in a pen.

Farmyard Fact!

Lambs have their own special areas in a pen, where ewes cannot go. The lambs stay here when they want to escape from their mums!

What do sheep eat?

Sheep graze, or chew, on grass. They eat a lot of food in a short time, and then they rest for a while.

During the summer, sheep can feed on fresh grass, but in winter the farmer gives them hay. Hay is dried grass.

⇩ Farmers clean the troughs every day, and fill them with fresh water.

⇧ Sheep have sharp teeth that can cut hay and grass.

Farmers also give the sheep food pellets, which are made of grains such as corn and oats. These food pellets contain lots of **vitamins**.

⇧ Pellets help sheep to grow big and strong.

Sheep need to drink a lot of water to stay healthy. They drink water out of **troughs**.

Troughs are normally long, ⇨ shallow and made of metal.

trough

Farmyard Fact!

Sheep spend around seven hours a day eating. Their favourite times to graze are early morning and late afternoon.

The life cycle of sheep

Most lambs are born in spring, when the weather is getting warmer and the grass has started to grow.

A ewe gives birth to one or two lambs at a time.

⇧ After the lamb is born, its mother licks it clean.

Farmyard Fact!

A lamb can find its mother in a flock by listening for her bleat. Every sheep's bleat sounds different.

3 ← Soon, it can stand up by itself and feed from its mother's milk.

↓ After a few days, the lambs can live in pens or outdoors. Then the life cycle begins again.

4

The daily life of sheep

Sheep spend most of their day walking, eating and resting.

Ewes and lambs stay together in a flock, but rams are kept away to stop them from fighting.

Farmers train **sheepdogs** to make the flock move towards the pasture, or into pens and shelters.

⇩ Sheepdogs are trained to stay behind a flock. They need to be both clever and gentle.

Vets visit the sheep and give them medicine when they are ill. They also give sheep a special bath, called a sheep-dip, to keep their skin healthy.

Farmers give their sheep medicines. ⇨
This stops them from getting ill.

Farmyard fact!

In some countries, sheep are kept on hills or mountains. **Shepherds** travel on horseback or on motorbikes to check that their flocks are safe.

Why do we farm sheep?

Most sheep are kept by farmers for their wool or their meat.

A farmer may choose some lambs that will grow to become ewes or rams. The others will be used for meat. Their meat is known as lamb.

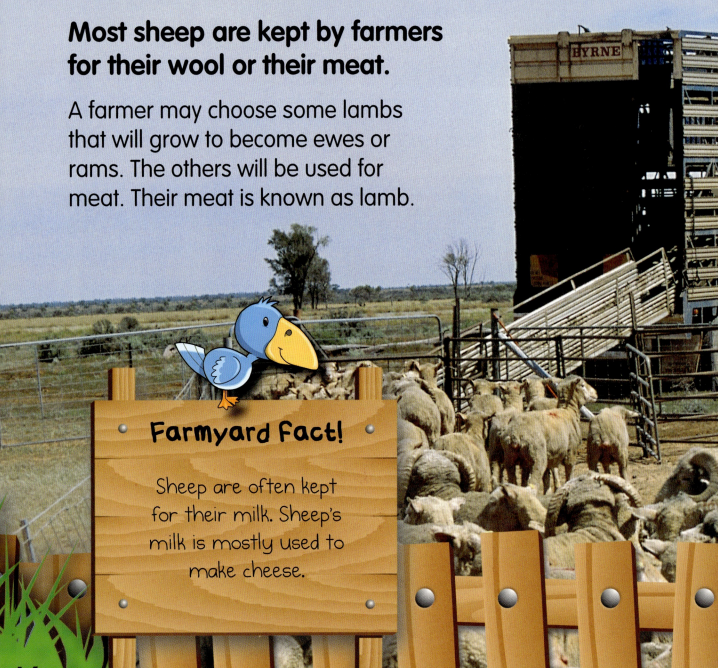

Farmyard Fact!

Sheep are often kept for their milk. Sheep's milk is mostly used to make cheese.

Sheep that are more than two years old are also used for meat. Their meat is called mutton.

These chops have come from lambs.

Farmers move their sheep on to a truck, so they can be taken to market.

Sheep shearing

At least once a year, sheep that are kept for their wool need to have a haircut.

Cutting the wool from a sheep is called shearing. Having no fur helps the sheep to stay cool in summer. Farmers use **shears**, or scissors, to cut the wool.

⇧ A farmer uses shears to remove the wool, without hurting the ewe.

Farmyard Fact!

A fleece is washed and combed before it is turned into woollen yarn. Special colourings, called dyes, are added to wool.

If the wool is removed in one piece, it is called a fleece. Most wool is used to make clothes and carpets.

Wool can be used to knit clothes and blankets.

After shearing, sheep look thin. Their wool starts to grow back straight away.

Breeds of sheep

Merino sheep

There are many different breeds, or kinds, of sheep. Most sheep are kept for either their meat or their wool.

Farmers keep merino sheep for their fine, soft wool. It is used to make clothes.

⇧ Merino ewes have white faces. They do not grow horns.

Farmyard Fact!

Little Portland lambs are born with orange-red wool. It changes colour to white or grey when they are a few months old.

Jacob sheep have black-and-white fleeces, and long horns. They are mostly kept by farmers for their meat.

Blackface sheep are mostly kept for their meat. They are very strong and can live on cold, rainy mountains.

⇩ Jacob sheep do not grow very thick winter coats.

Jacob sheep

⇩ The wool from blackface sheep is strong. It can be used to make carpets.

Blackface sheep

Glossary

Pasture
This is a field of grass where animals, such as cows and sheep, can graze.

Pen
A pen is a small area that is surrounded with a fence. Animals are kept in pens.

Shears
Shears are tools used for cutting the fur, or wool, from a sheep's body.

Sheepdog
Sheepdogs are dogs that have been trained to move flocks of sheep.

Shepherd
A shepherd is a person who looks after sheep.

Trough
A trough is a long, narrow container that is used for giving an animal food or water.

Vitamin
Vitamins are found in food. They help animals, and people, to grow well and stay healthy.

Index

birth 12
Blackface sheep 21
bleat 5, 12
breeds 20

cheese 16

eating 10, 11, 14
ewes 7, 9, 12, 14, 16, 18, 20

feet 4
fields 8
fleece 18, 19, 21
flocks 6, 7, 12, 14, 15
fur 4, 18

grass 10
grazing 10, 11

hay 10
hooves 4
horns 5, 7, 21

Jacob sheep 21

lamb chops 17
lambs 6, 7, 9, 12, 13, 14, 16
Little Portland lambs 20

mammals 4
market 17
meat 6, 16, 17, 21
medicines 15
Merino sheep 20
milk 4, 6, 13, 16
mutton 17

pastures 8, 14, 22
pellets 11
pens 9, 13, 14, 22
rams 5, 7, 14, 16

shearing 18, 19
sheep-dip 15
sheepdogs 14, 22
shelters 14
shepherds 15, 22

trough 11, 22

vets 15
vitamins 11, 22

water 10, 11
wool 4, 6, 16, 18, 19, 20

23

Notes for parents and teachers

- Talk about the basic needs that animals and humans share, such as food, space and shelter. Encourage the child to think about how wild animals get their food and find shelter.

- It is fun to find ways that animals are similar, or different to one another – and observing these things is a core science skill. Children could draw pictures of animals with four legs, or ones that eat plants, for example, and go on to identify those that are both plant-eaters and four-legged.

- Be prepared for questions about how animals become the meat that we eat. It helps children understand this part of the food chain if they can see it in context: all animals live and die, and farm animals are bred for this purpose.

- Cooking together is a great opportunity to have fun and learn. Following a recipe allows children to practise their reading and measuring skills, follow instructions, chat and be creative. Point out the ways that food changes as ingredients are mixed, heated or cooled. Talk about eating a balanced diet, and the benefits we receive from the different food groups, including meat, milk and eggs.